Christmas Songs
for Fingerstyle Guitar

T0088547

PLAYBACK+
Speed • Pitch • Balance • Loop

To access audio visit:
www.halleonard.com/mylibrary

Enter Code
6290-0463-9968-1277

Arranged by Pete Billmann
Recorded by Doug Boduch

ISBN 978-1-5400-5914-7

Visit Hal Leonard Online at
www.halleonard.com

Contact us:
Hal Leonard
7777 West Bluemound Road
Milwaukee, WI 53213
Email: info@halleonard.com

In Europe, contact:
Hal Leonard Europe Limited
42 Wigmore Street
Marylebone, London, W1U 2RN
Email: info@halleonardeurope.com

In Australia, contact:
Hal Leonard Australia Pty. Ltd.
4 Lentara Court
Cheltenham, Victoria, 3192 Australia
Email: info@halleonard.com.au

All I Want for Christmas Is My Two Front Teeth

Words and Music by Don Gardner

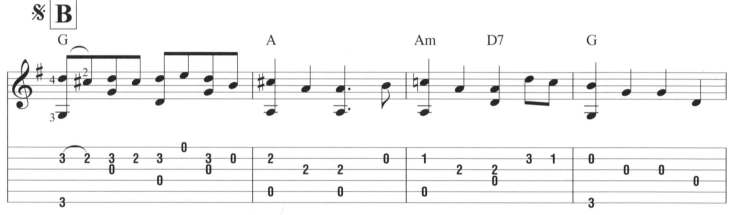

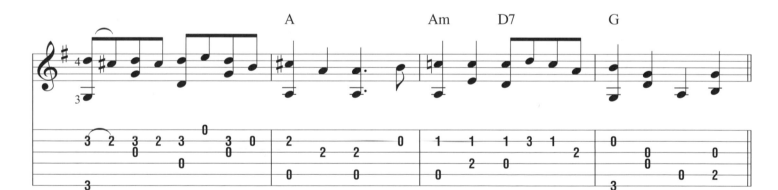

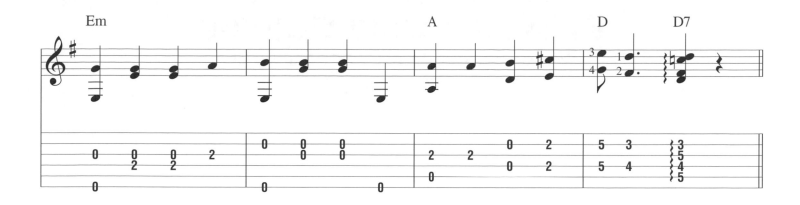

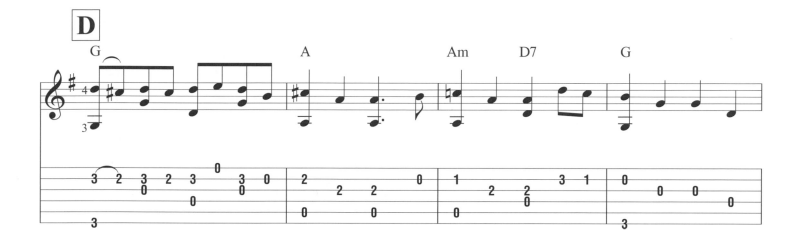

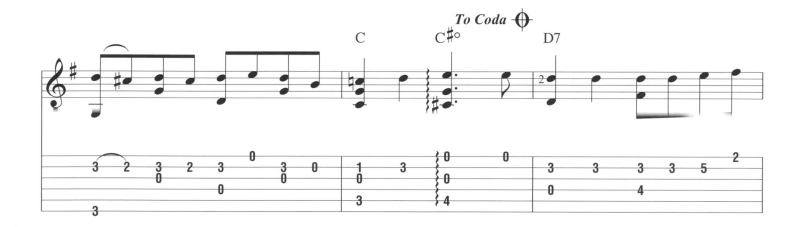

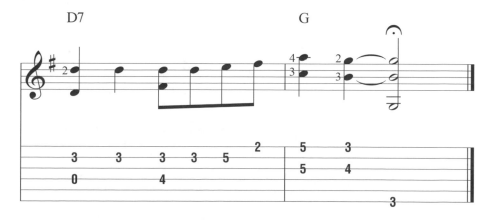

Baby, It's Cold Outside

from the Motion Picture NEPTUNE'S DAUGHTER

By Frank Loesser

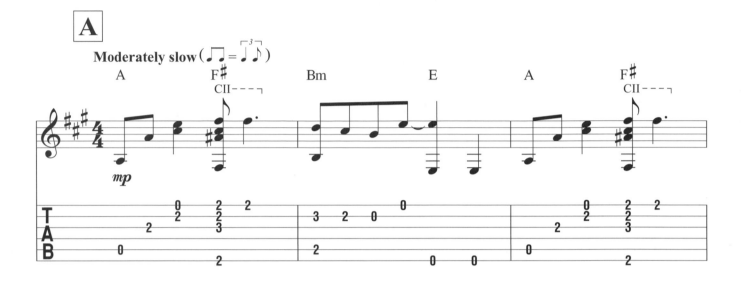

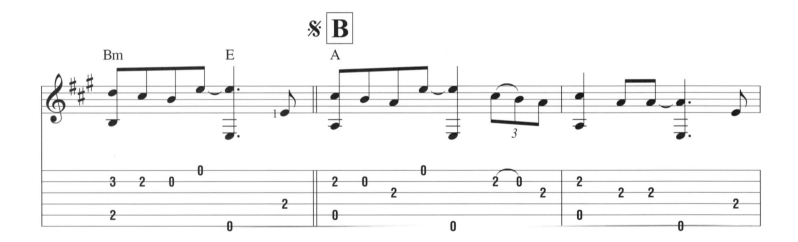

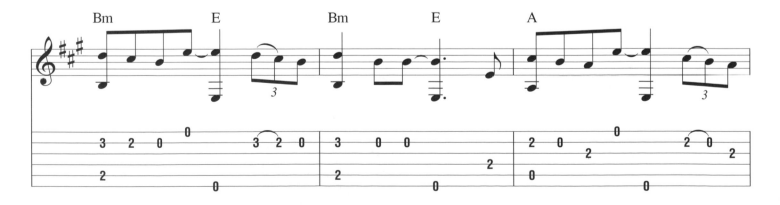

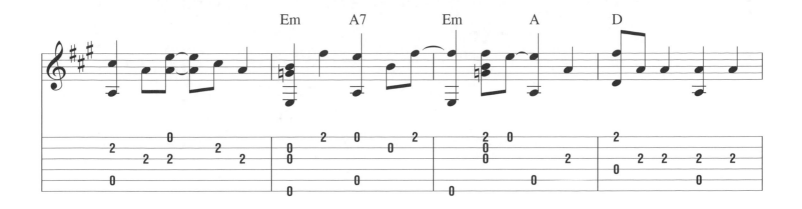

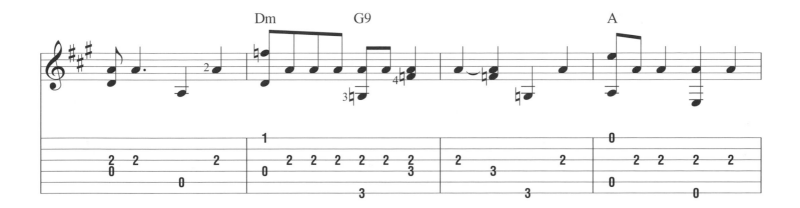

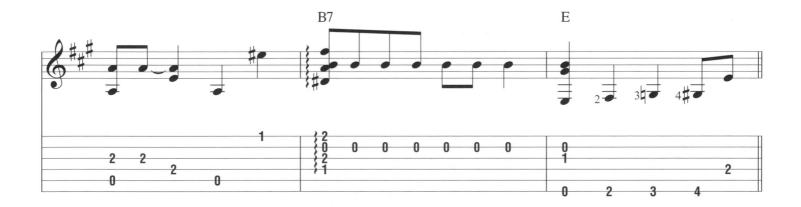

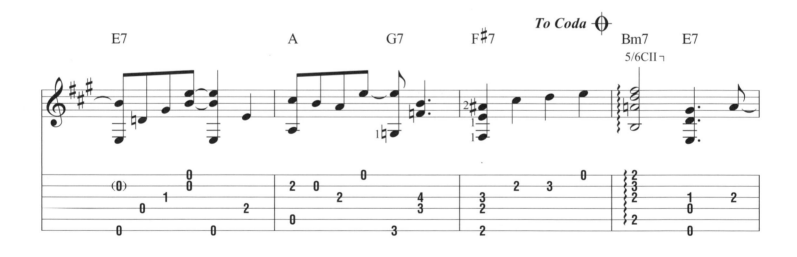

The Christmas Song
(Chestnuts Roasting on an Open Fire)

Music and Lyric by Mel Torme and Robert Wells

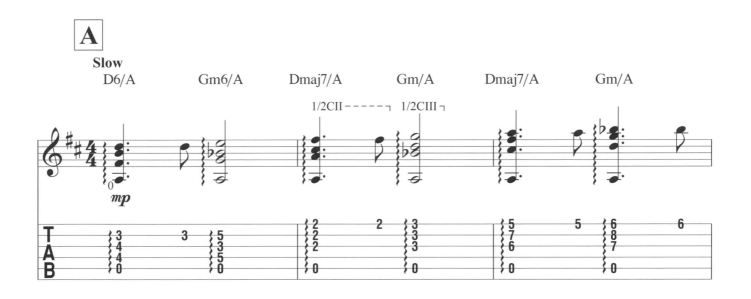

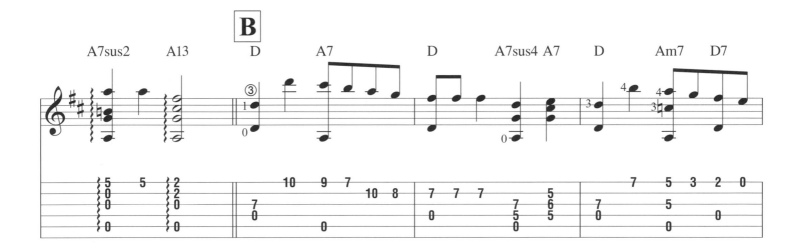

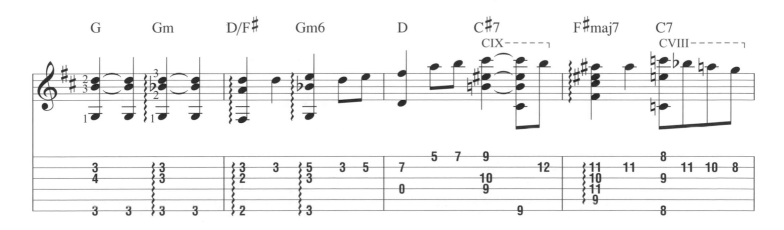

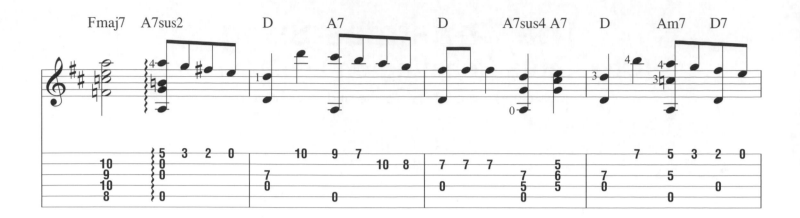

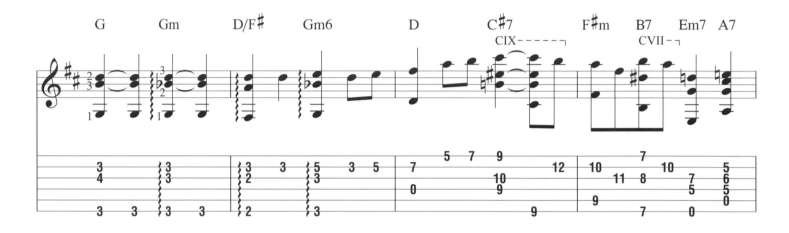

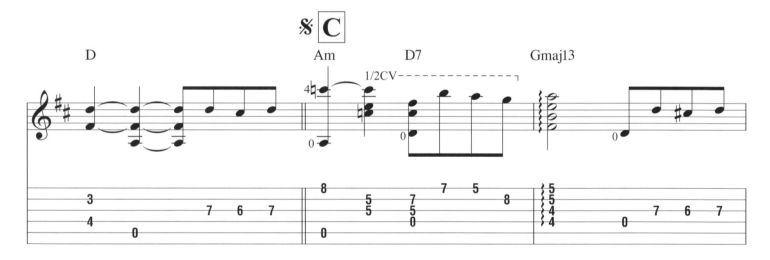

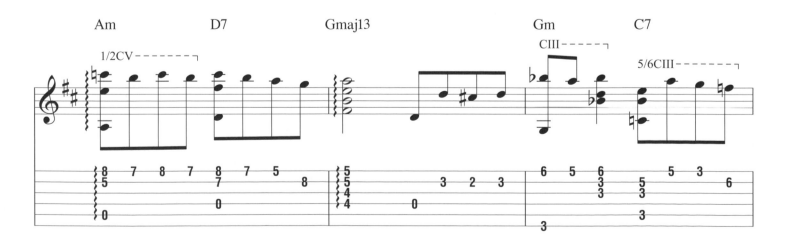

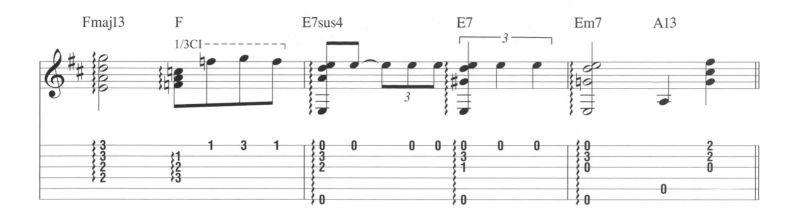

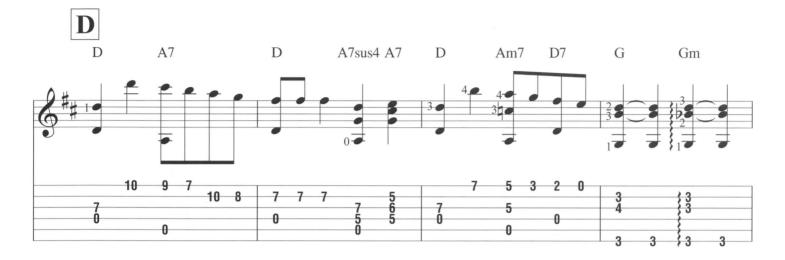

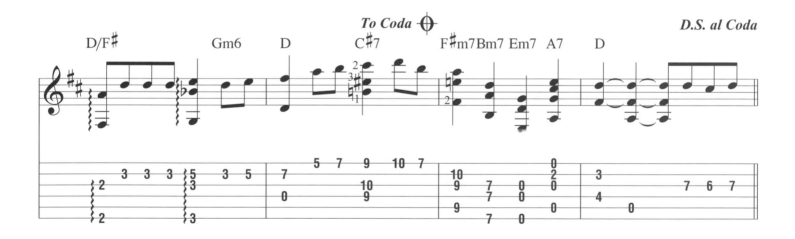

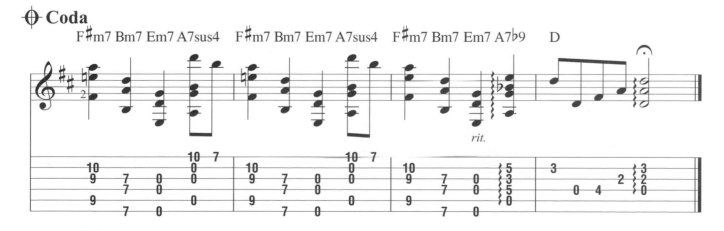

Blue Christmas

Words and Music by Billy Hayes and Jay Johnson

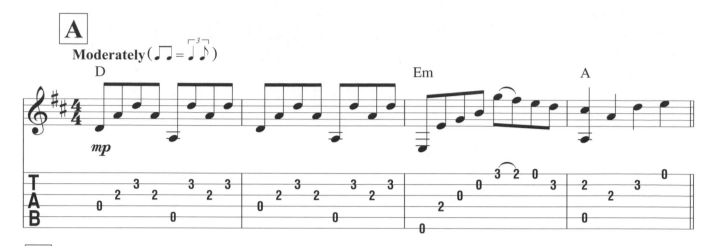

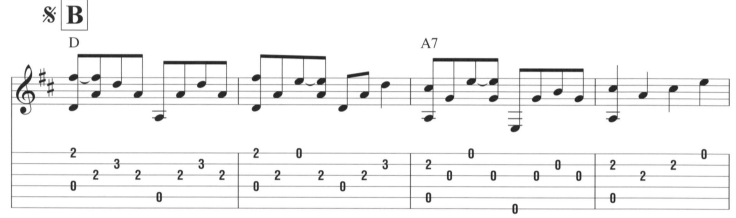

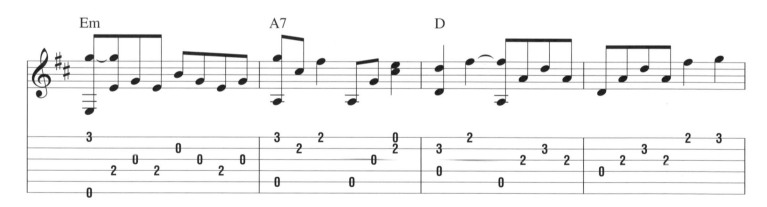

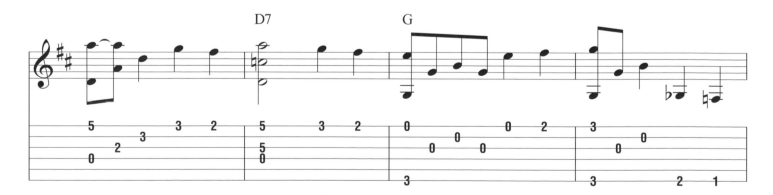

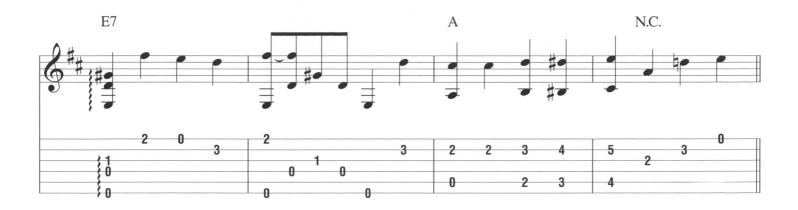

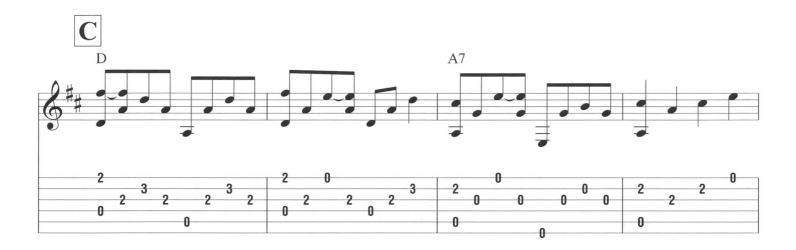

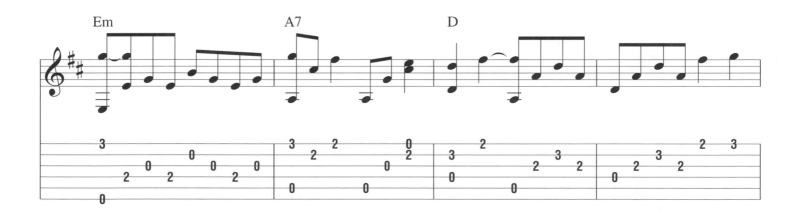

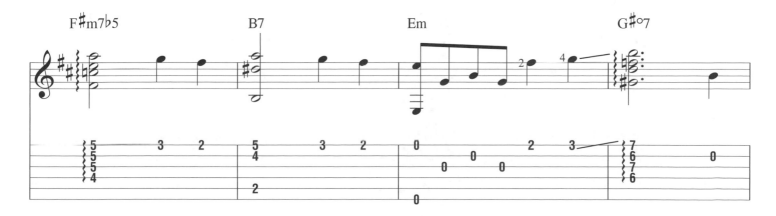

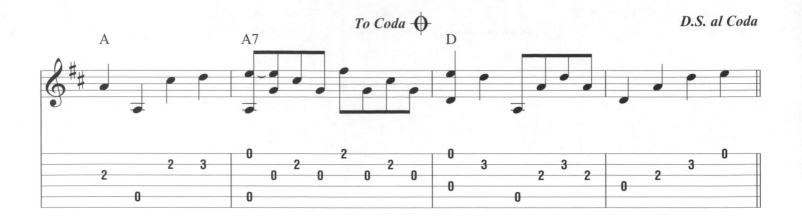

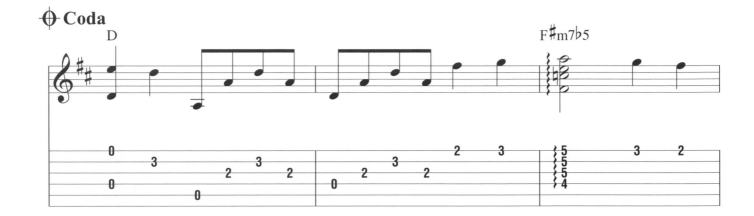

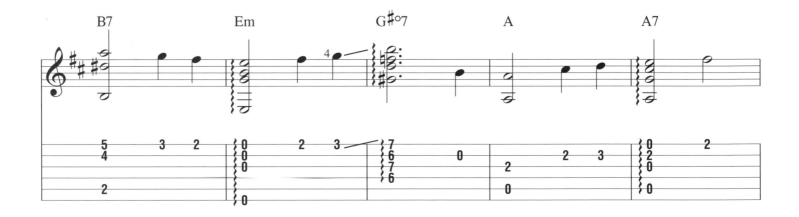

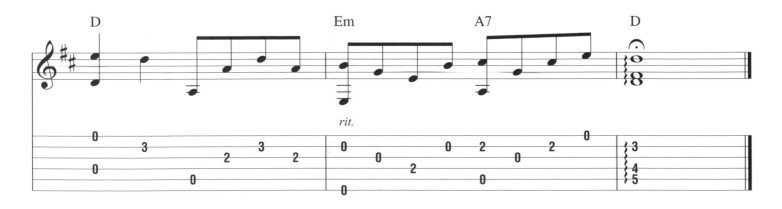

Christmas Time Is Here

from A CHARLIE BROWN CHRISTMAS

Words by Lee Mendelson
Music by Vince Guaraldi

*Harp harmonics produced by lightly touching strings
12 frets above fretted notes while picking strings.

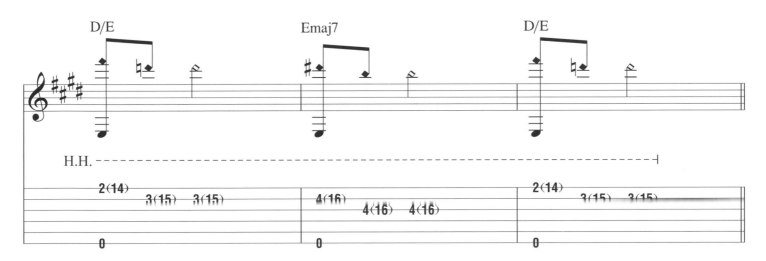

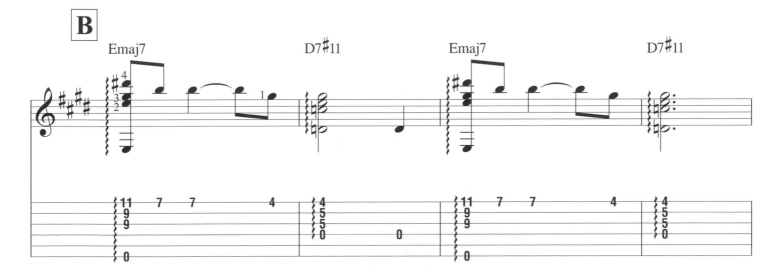

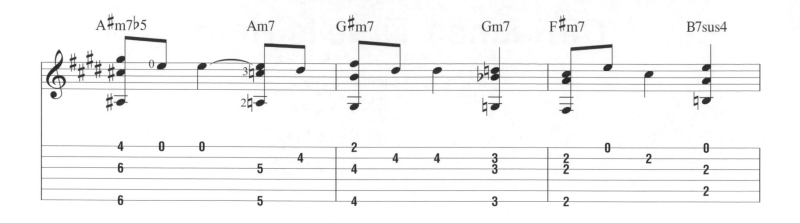

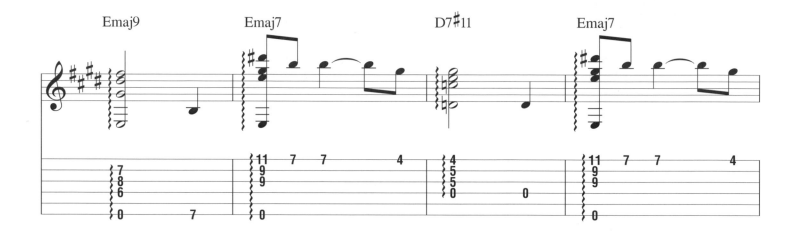

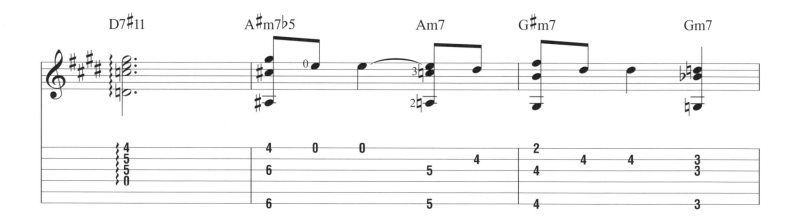

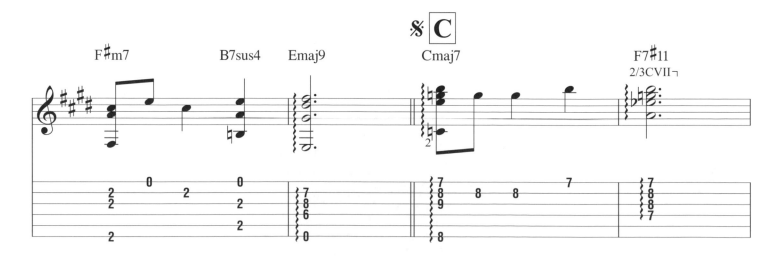

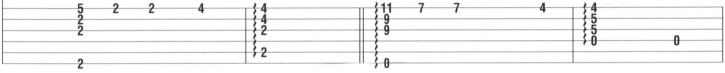

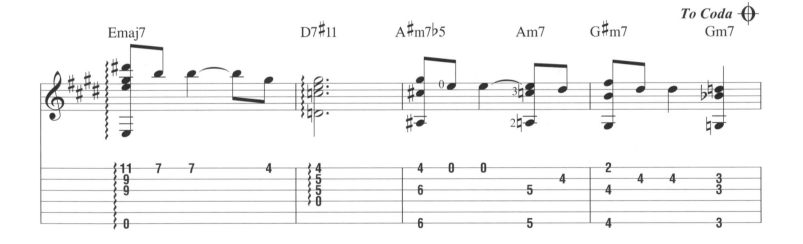

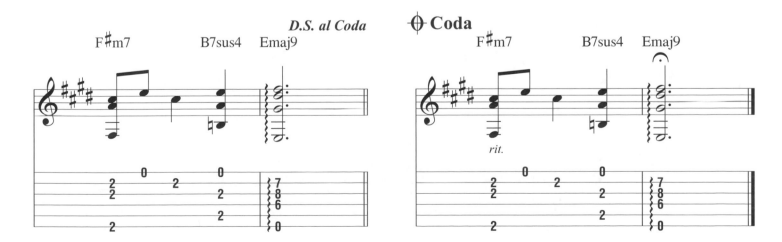

Frosty the Snow Man

Words and Music by Steve Nelson and Jack Rollins

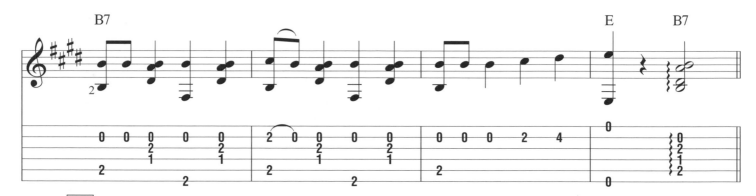

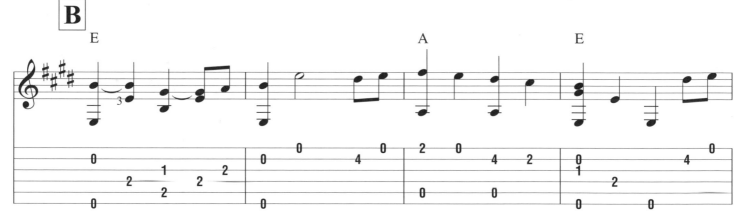

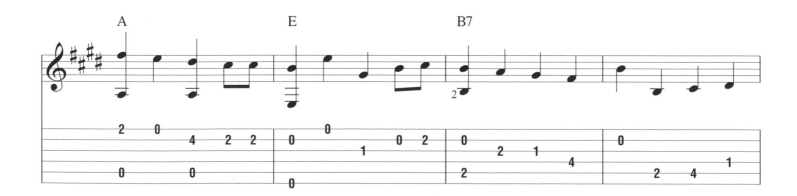

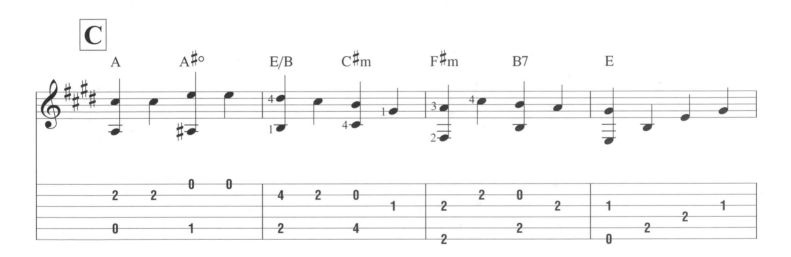

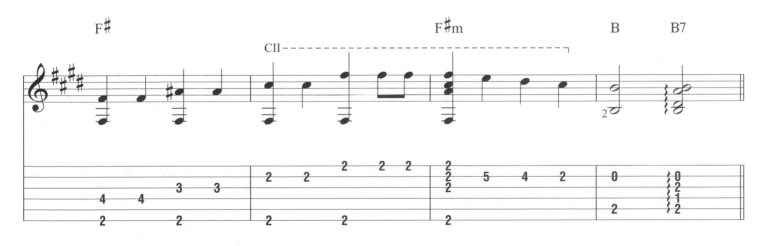

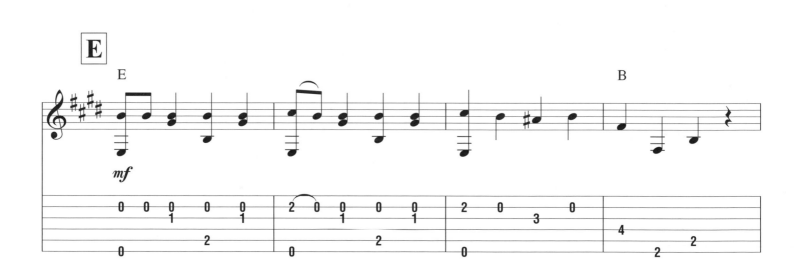

Have Yourself a Merry Little Christmas

from MEET ME IN ST. LOUIS

Words and Music by Hugh Martin and Ralph Blane

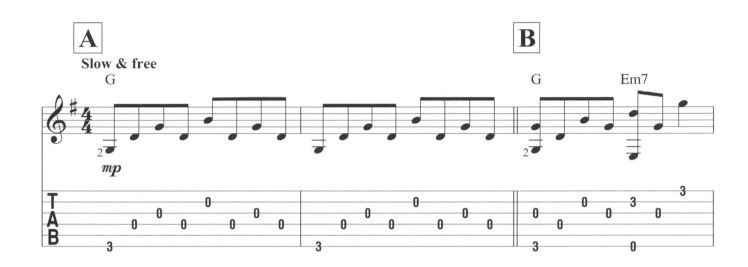

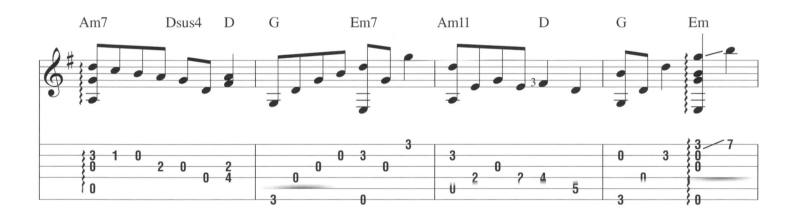

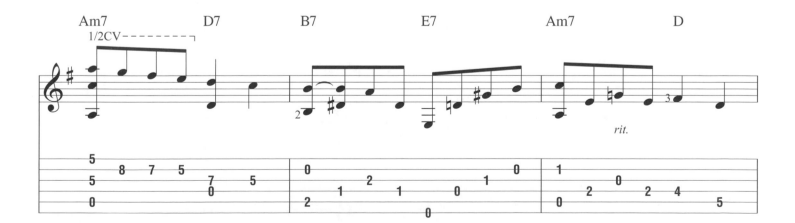

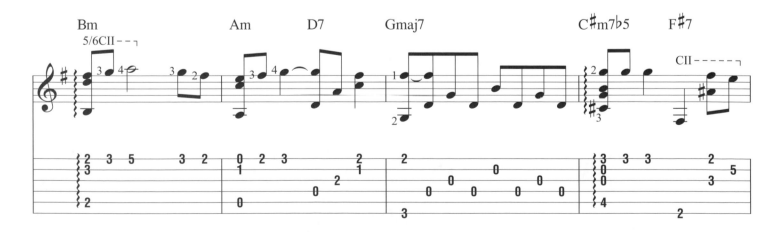

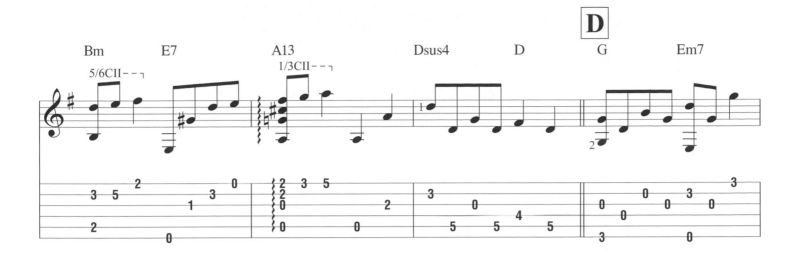

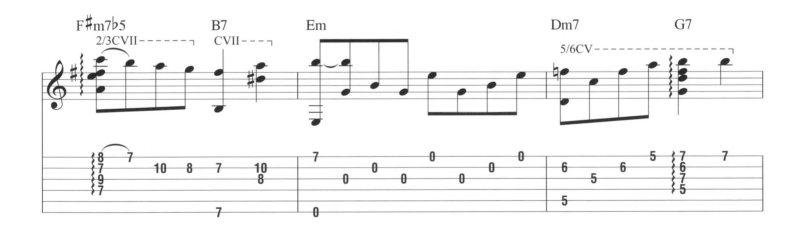

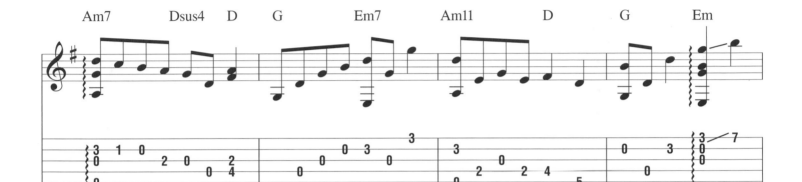

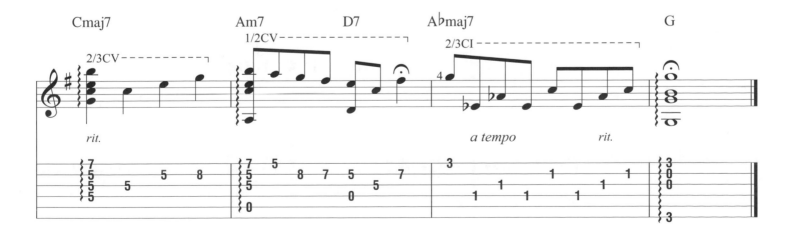

Here Comes Santa Claus
(Right Down Santa Claus Lane)

Words and Music by Gene Autry and Oakley Haldeman

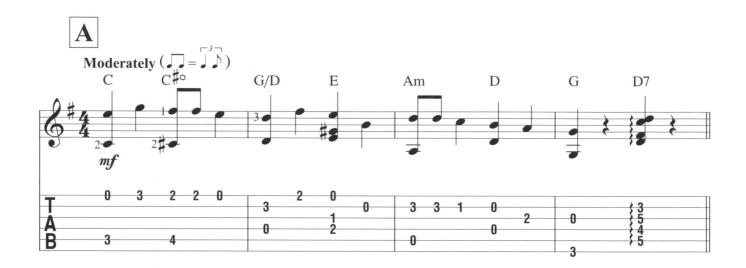

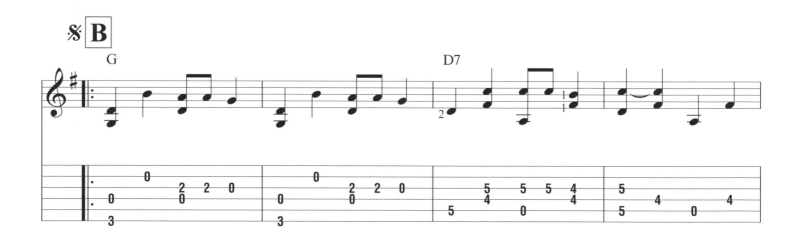

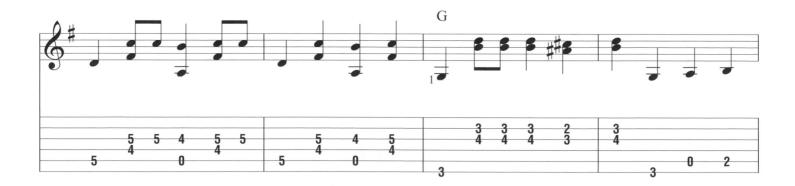

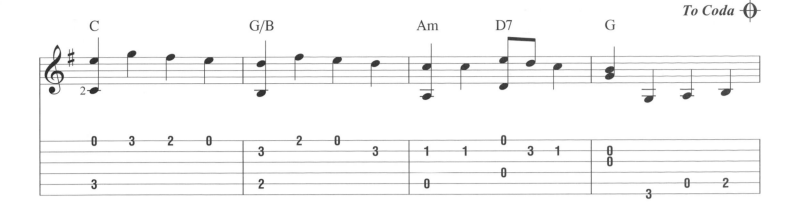

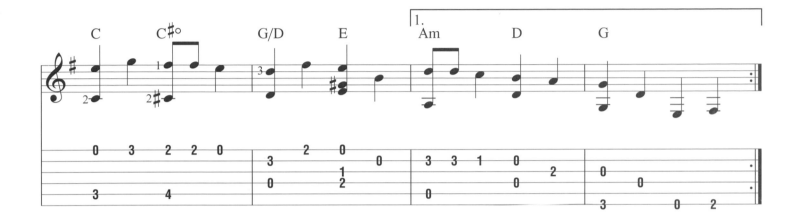

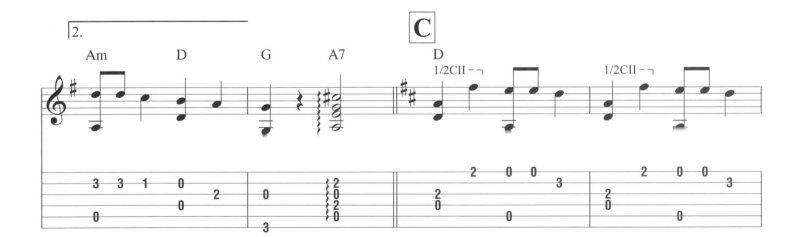

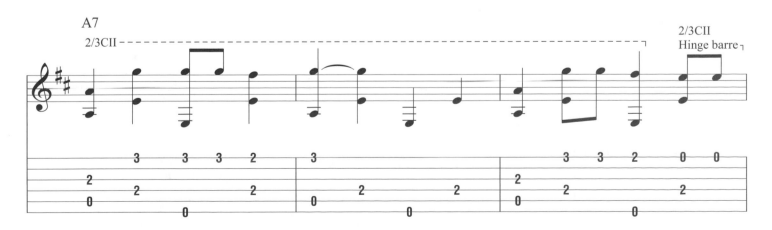

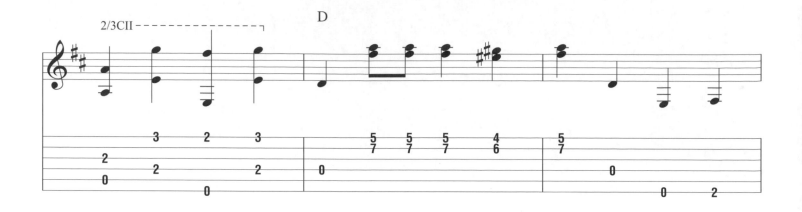

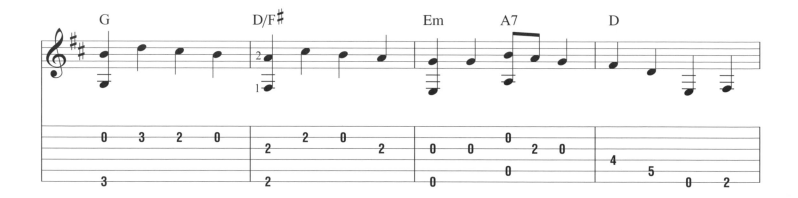

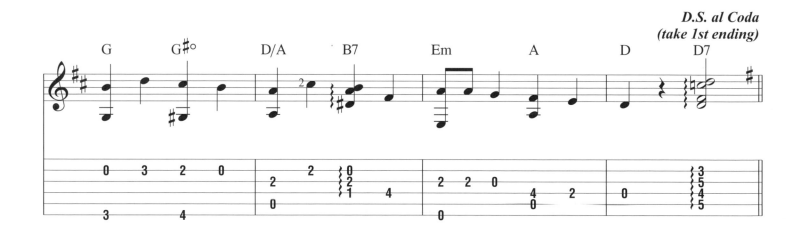

A Holly Jolly Christmas

Music and Lyrics by Johnny Marks

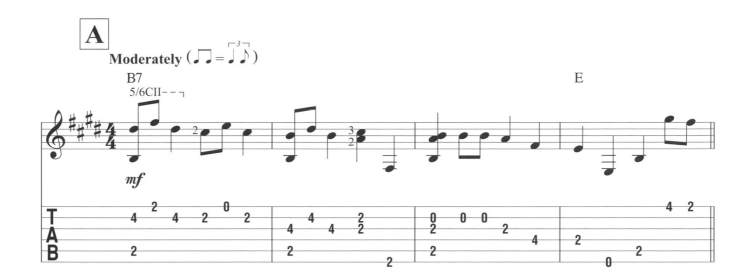

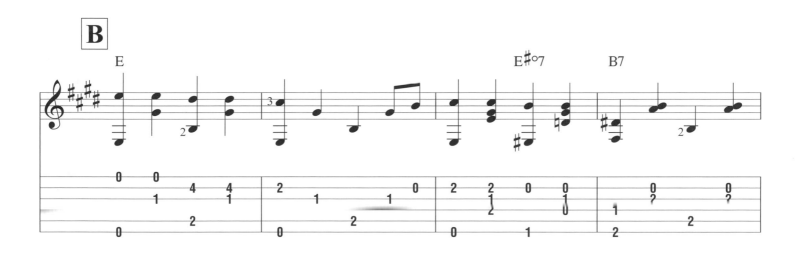

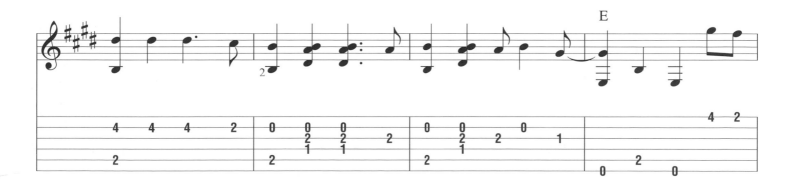

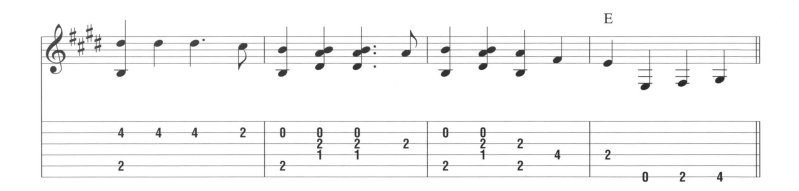

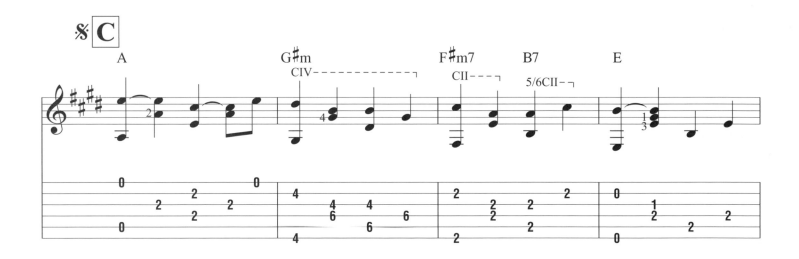

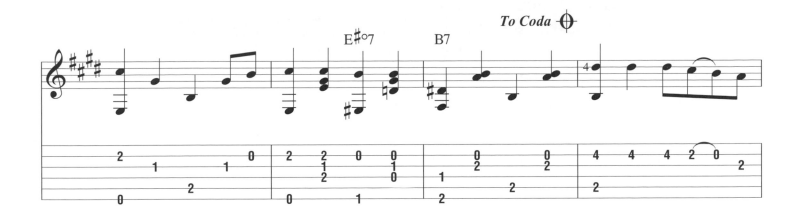

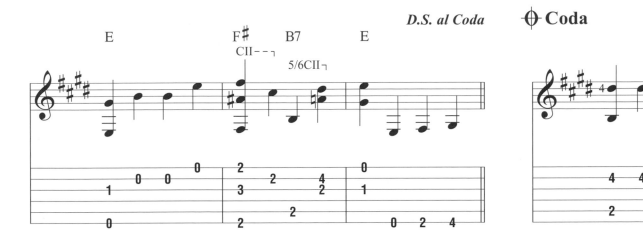

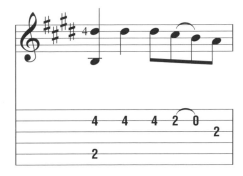

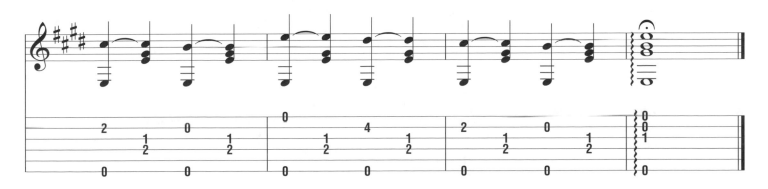

I'll Be Home for Christmas

Words and Music by Kim Gannon and Walter Kent

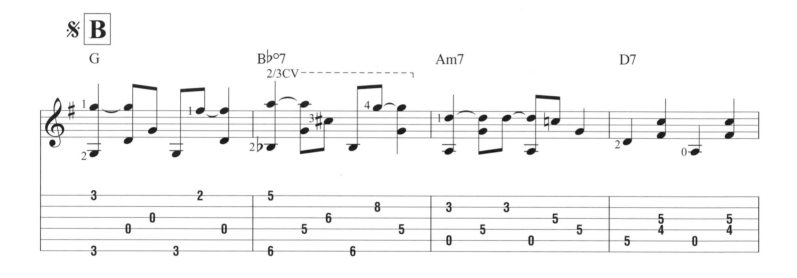

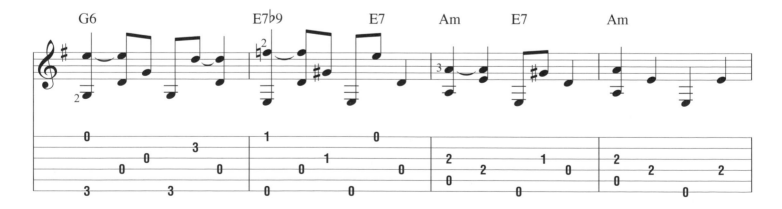

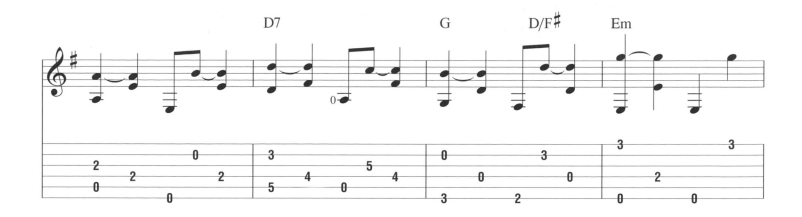

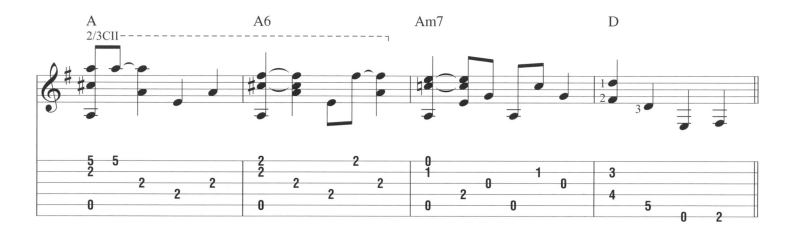

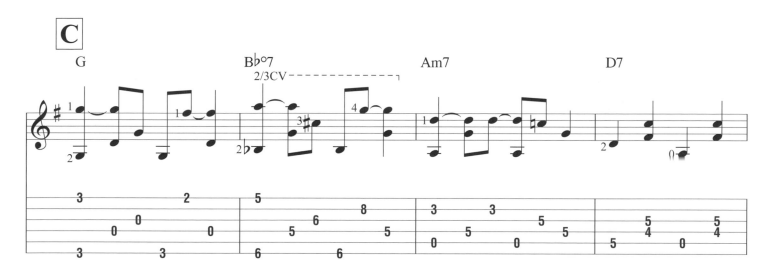

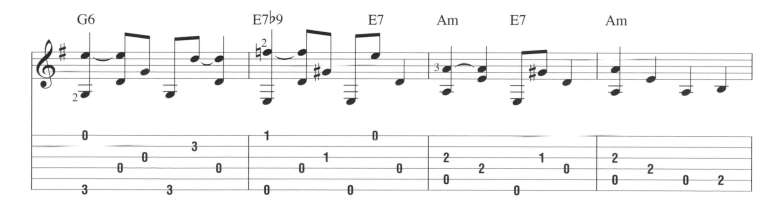

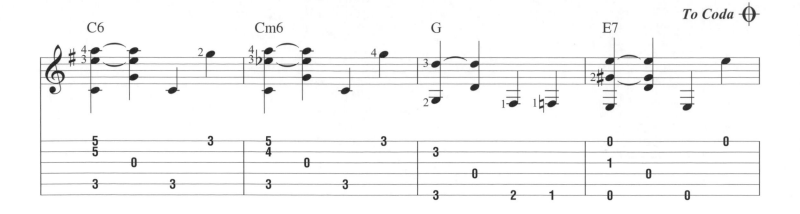

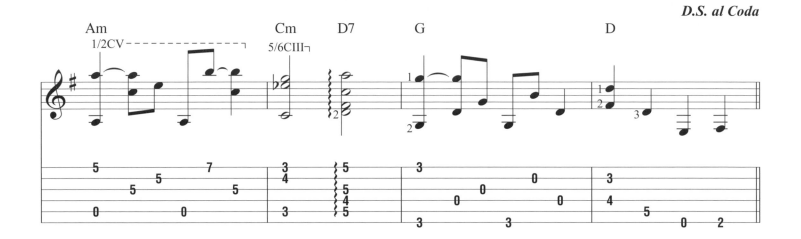

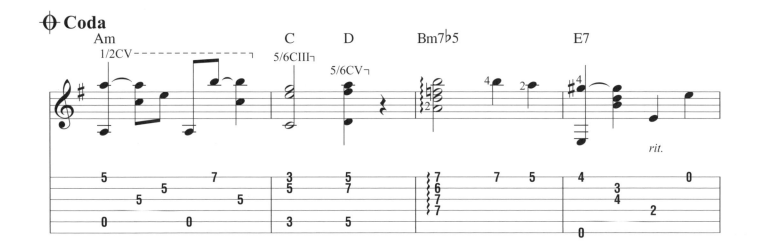

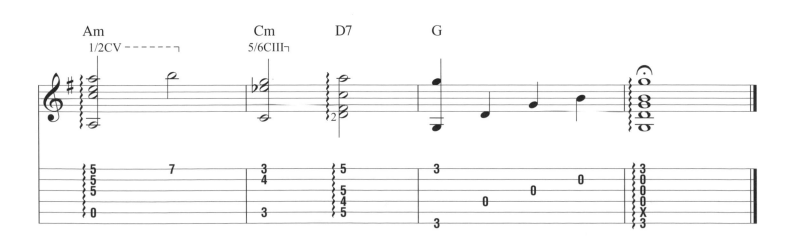

Let It Snow! Let It Snow! Let It Snow!

Words by Sammy Cahn
Music by Jule Styne

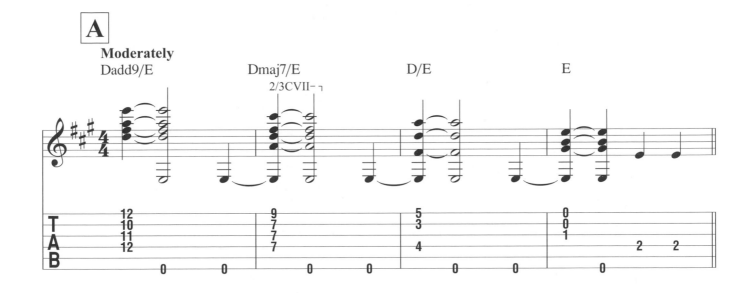

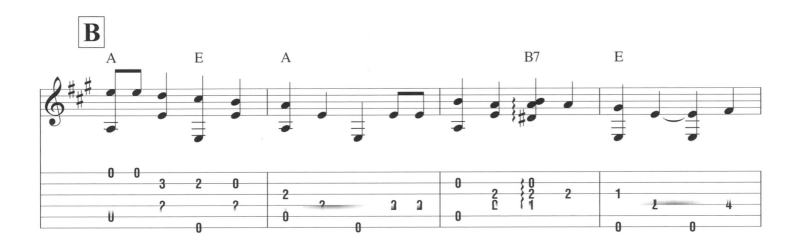

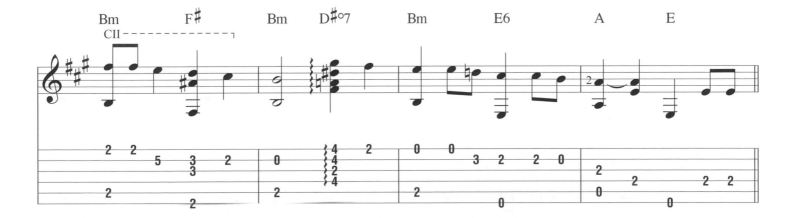

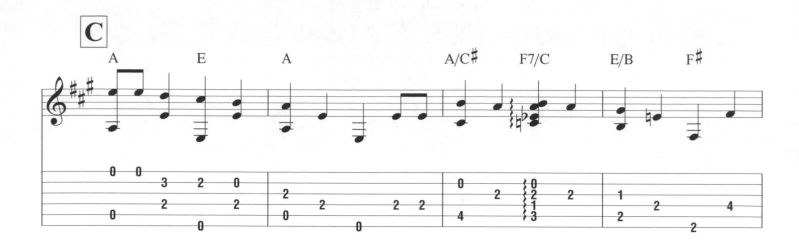

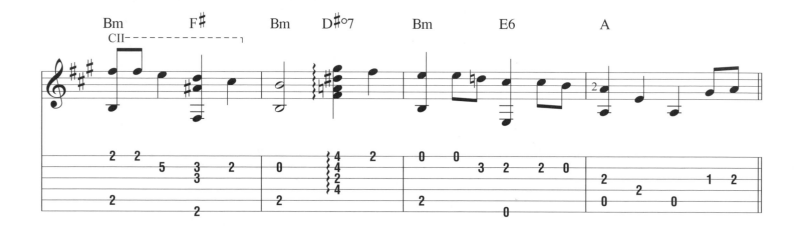

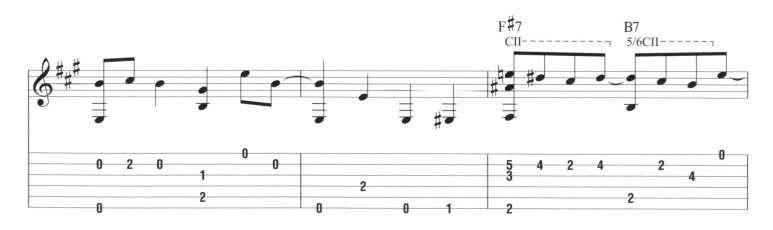

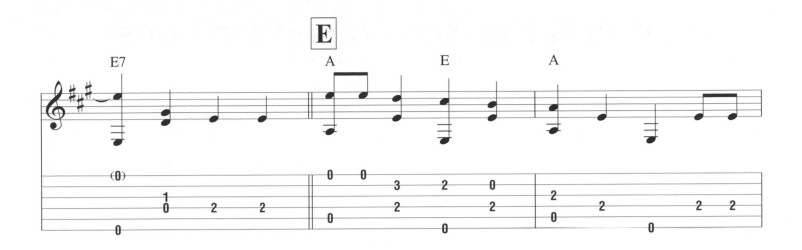

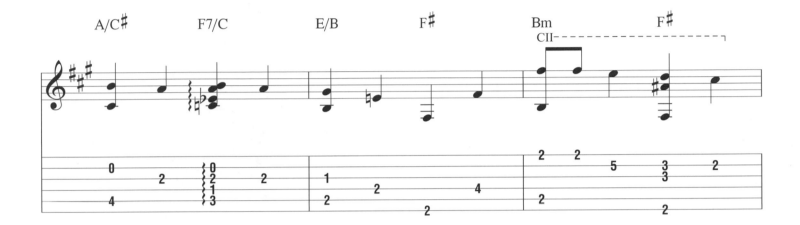

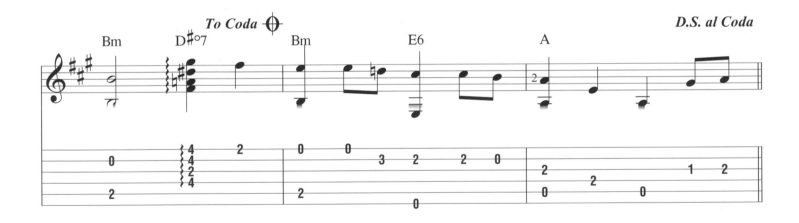

Rudolph the Red-Nosed Reindeer

Music and Lyrics by Johnny Marks

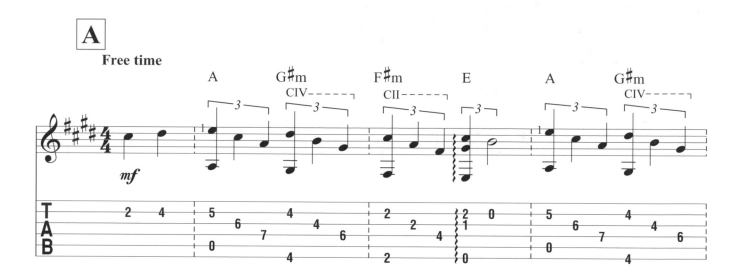

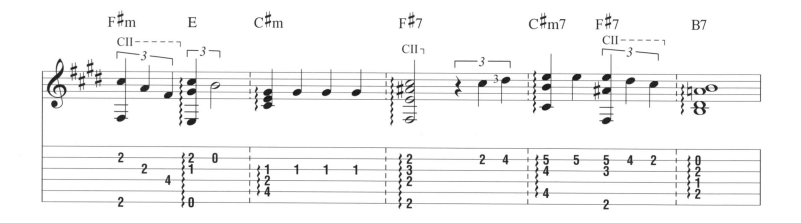

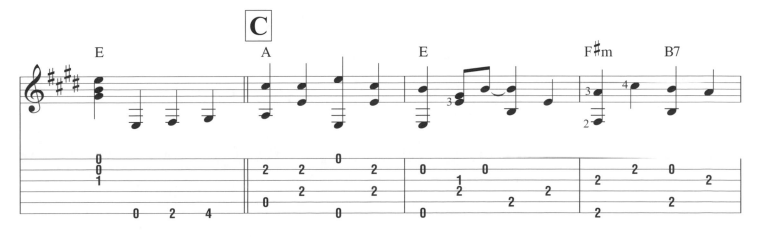

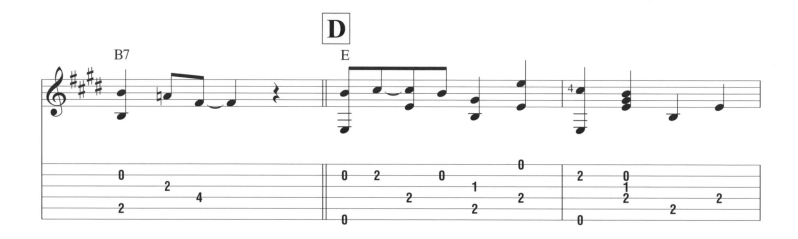

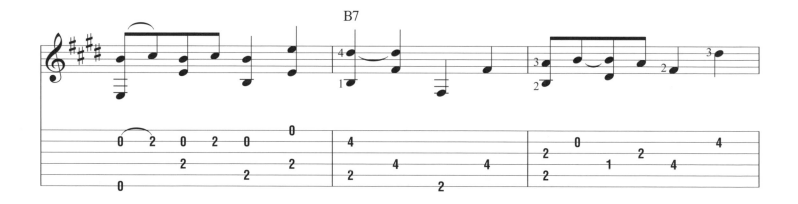

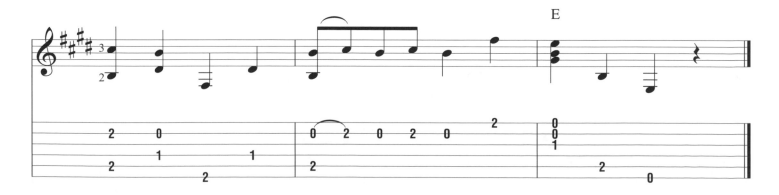

Silver and Gold

Music and Lyrics by Johnny Marks

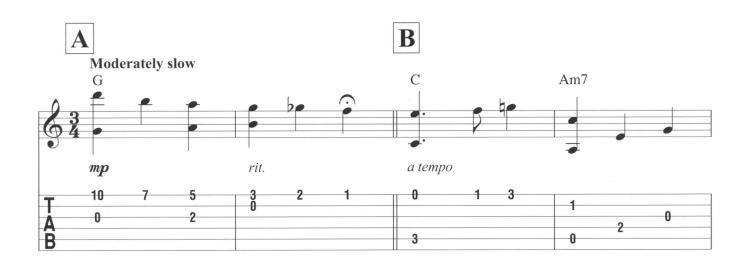

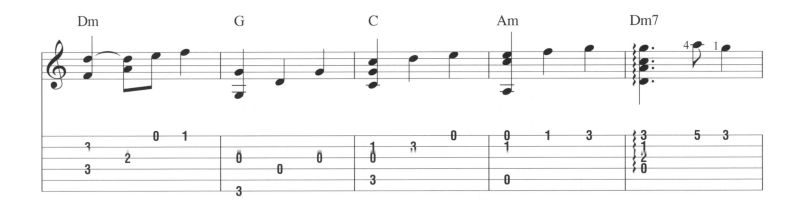

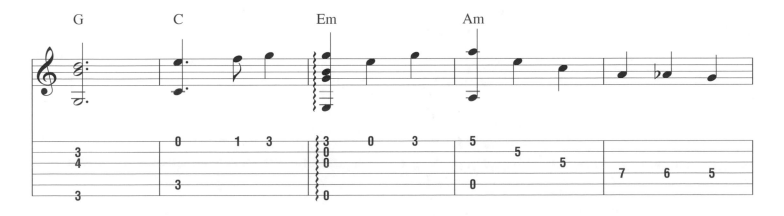

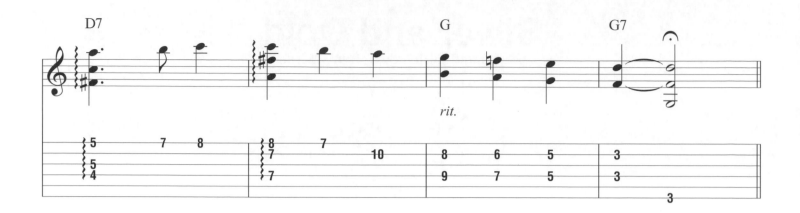

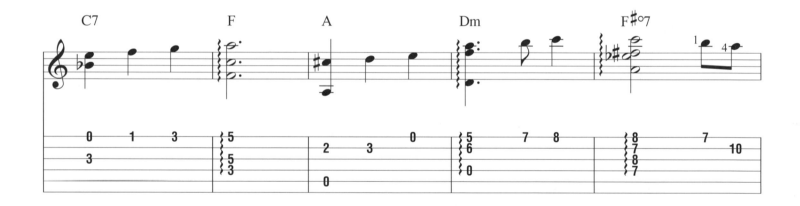

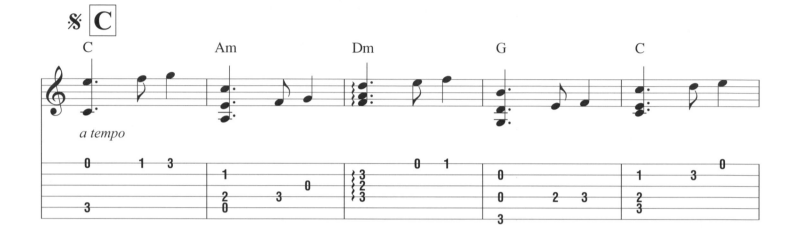

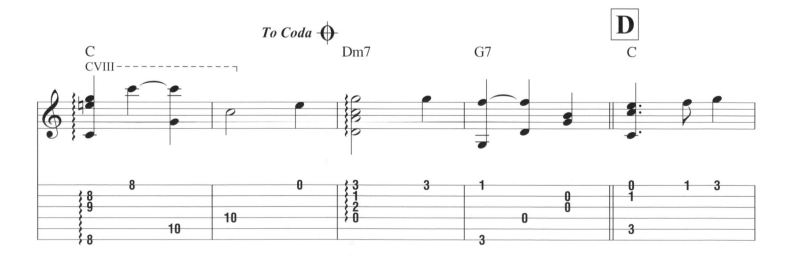

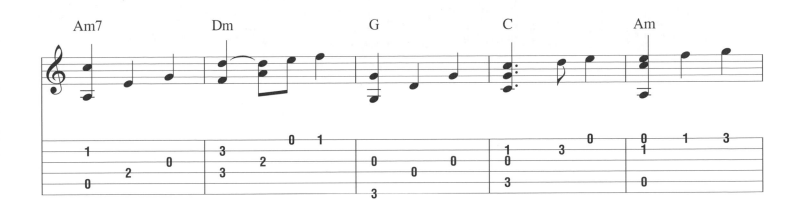

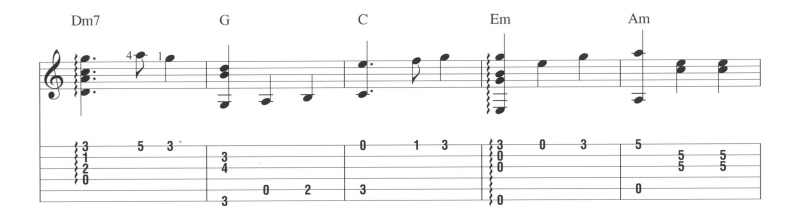

D.S. al Coda

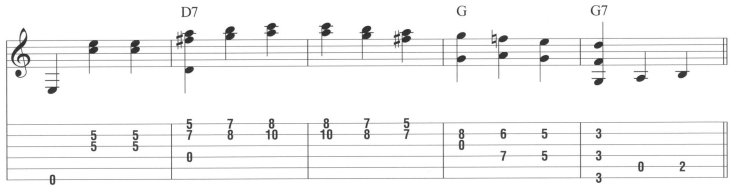

✆ Coda

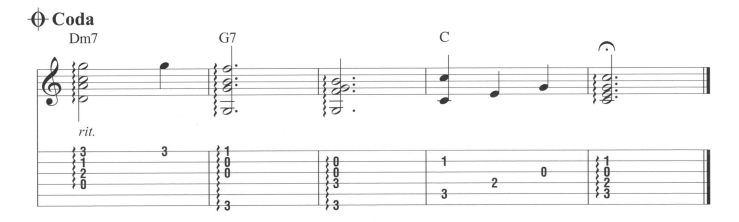

Santa Claus Is Comin' to Town

Words by Haven Gillespie
Music by J. Fred Coots

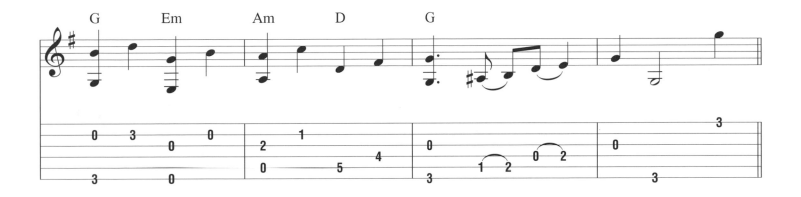

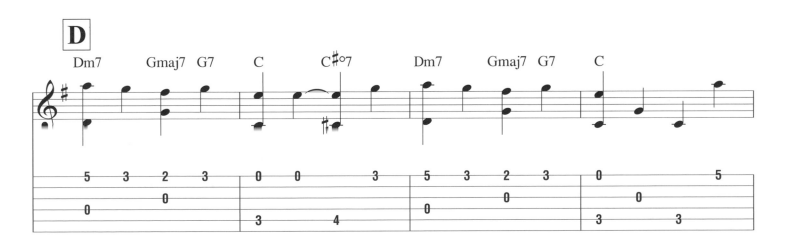

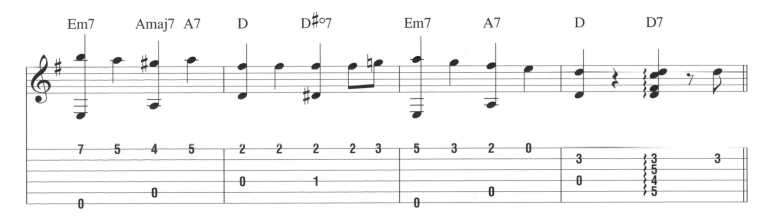

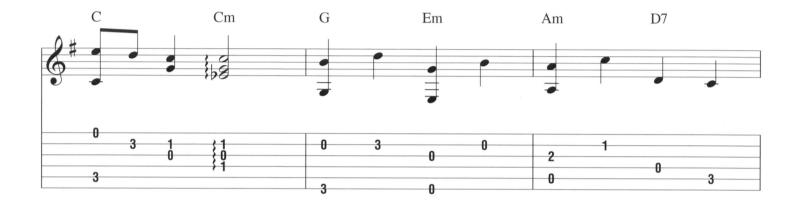

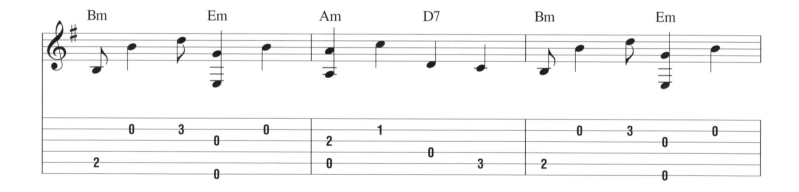

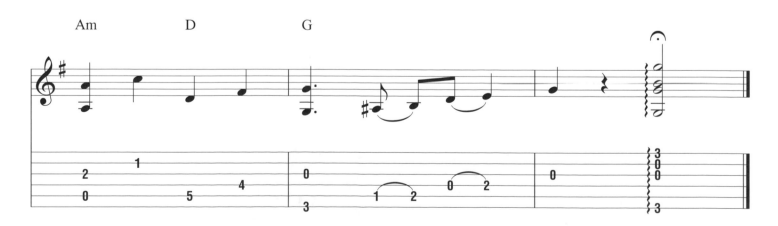

(There's No Place Like) Home for the Holidays

Words and Music by Al Stillman and Robert Allen

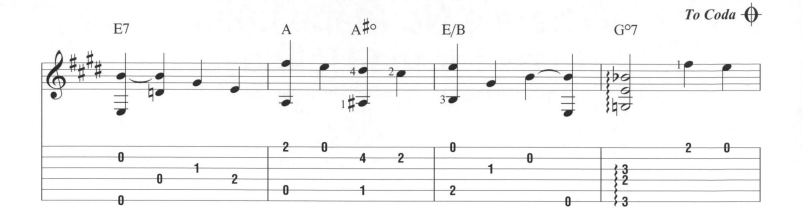

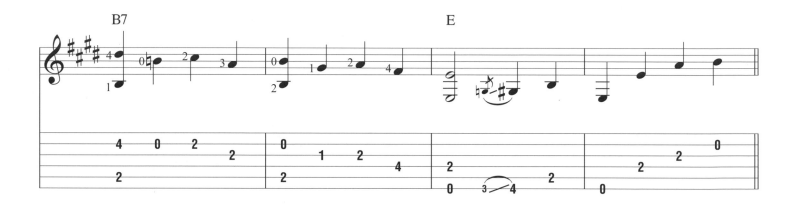

C

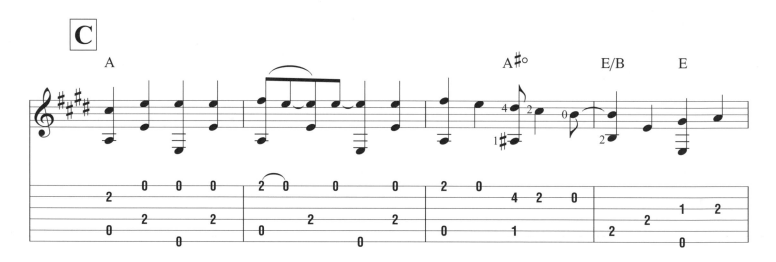

46

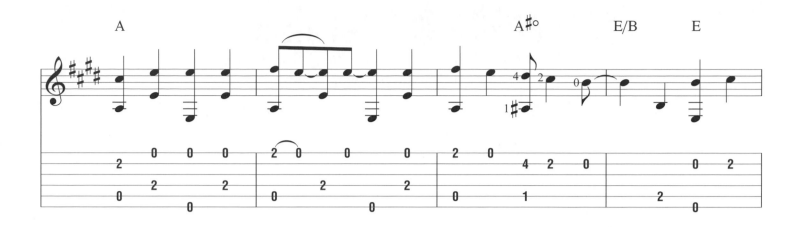

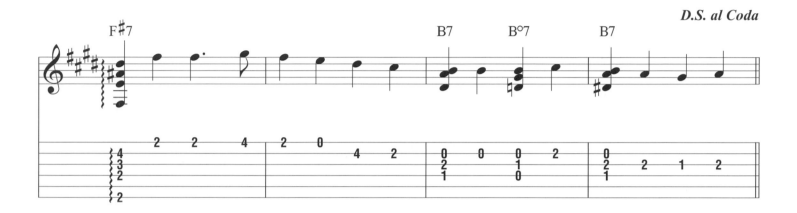

D.S. al Coda

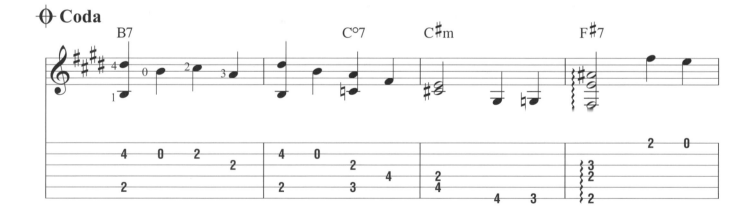

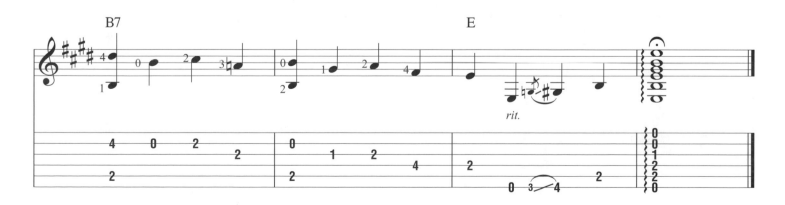

White Christmas

from the Motion Picture Irving Berlin's HOLIDAY INN

Words and Music by Irving Berlin

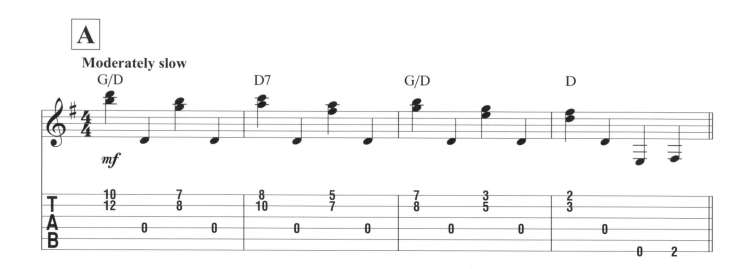

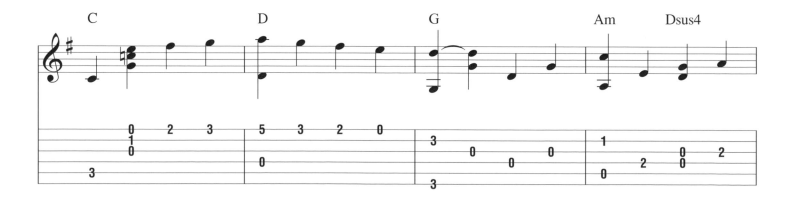

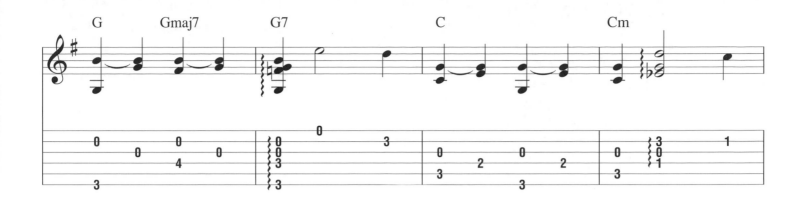

C

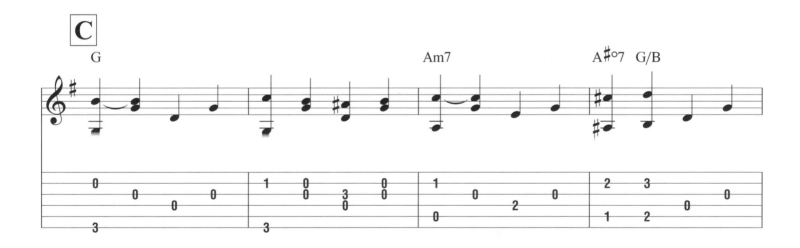

To Coda ⊕

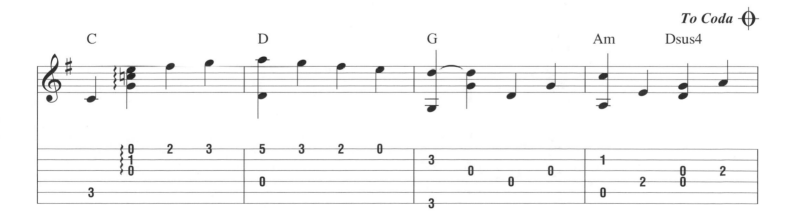

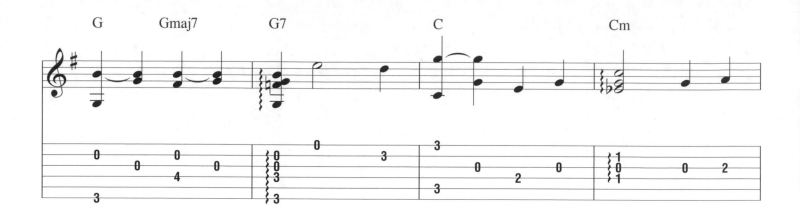

D.S. al Coda

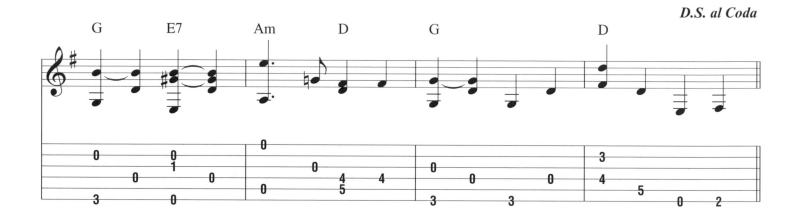

⊕ Coda

Slower

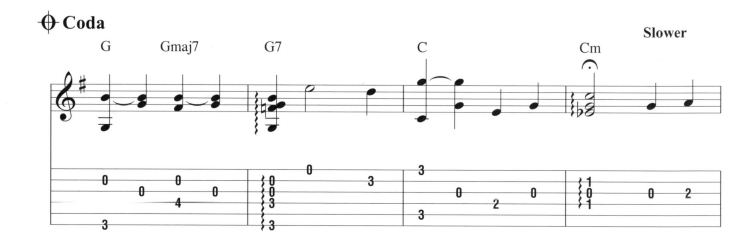

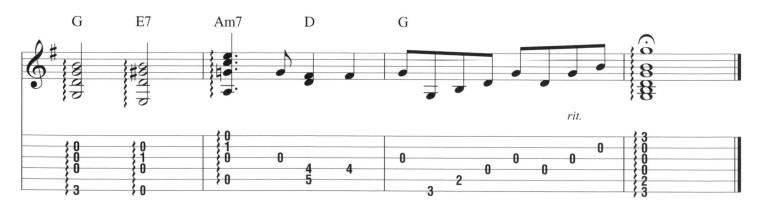

rit.

Winter Wonderland

Words by Dick Smith
Music by Felix Bernard

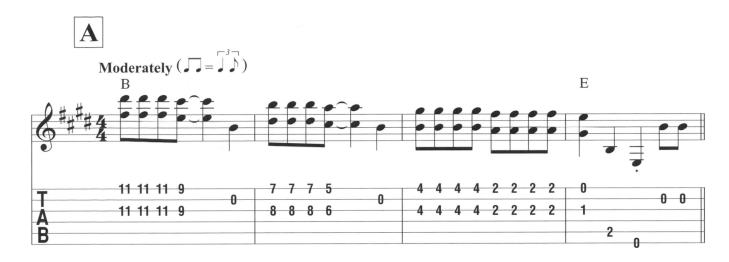

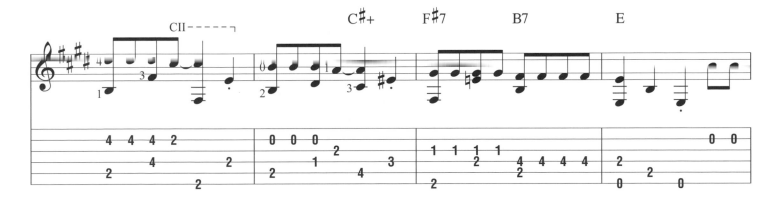

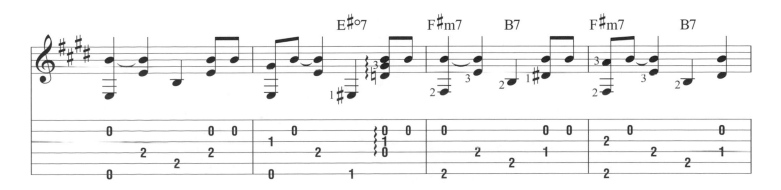

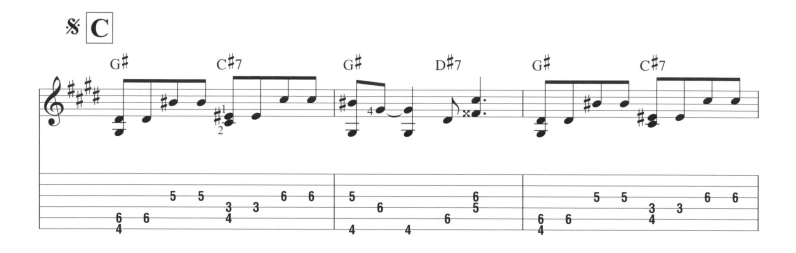

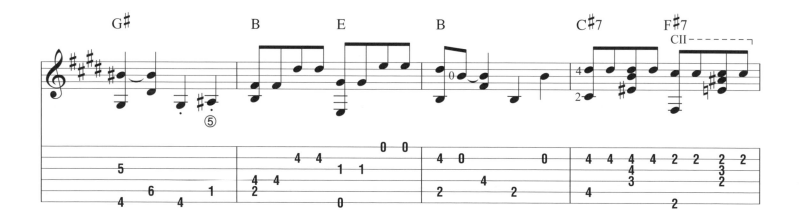

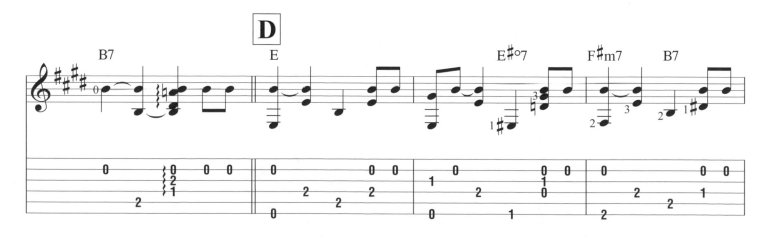

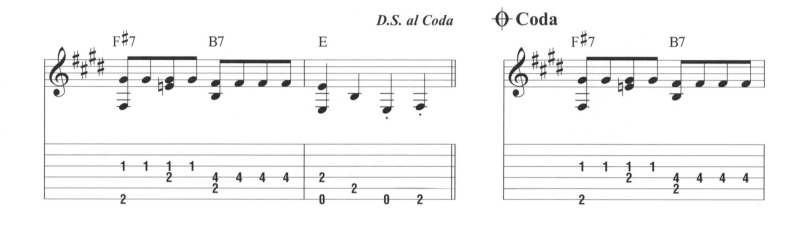

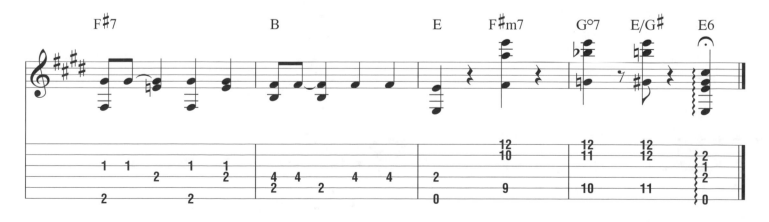

Celebrate Christmas
WITH YOUR GUITAR AND HAL LEONARD

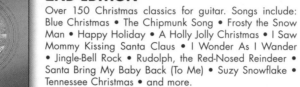

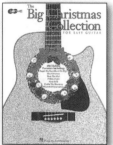 

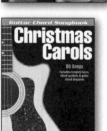 

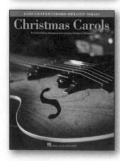

THE BEST CHRISTMAS GUITAR FAKE BOOK EVER – 2ND EDITION
INCLUDES TAB

Over 150 Christmas classics for guitar. Songs include: Blue Christmas • The Chipmunk Song • Frosty the Snow Man • Happy Holiday • A Holly Jolly Christmas • I Saw Mommy Kissing Santa Claus • I Wonder As I Wander • Jingle-Bell Rock • Rudolph, the Red-Nosed Reindeer • Santa Bring My Baby Back (To Me) • Suzy Snowflake • Tennessee Christmas • and more.

00240053 Melody/Lyrics/Chords $25.00

THE BIG CHRISTMAS COLLECTION FOR EASY GUITAR

Includes over 70 Christmas favorites, such as: Ave Maria • Blue Christmas • Deck the Hall • Feliz Navidad • Frosty the Snow Man • Happy Holiday • A Holly Jolly Christmas • Joy to the World • O Holy Night • Silver and Gold • Suzy Snowflake • and more. Does not include TAB.

00698978 Easy Guitar $17.99

CHRISTMAS
INCLUDES TAB

Guitar Play-Along Volume 22
Book/Online Audio

8 songs: The Christmas Song (Chestnuts Roasting on an Open Fire) • Frosty the Snow Man • Happy Xmas (War Is Over) • Here Comes Santa Claus (Right Down Santa Claus Lane) • Jingle-Bell Rock • Merry Christmas, Darling • Rudolph the Red-Nosed Reindeer • Silver Bells.

00699600 Guitar Tab $15.99

CHRISTMAS CAROLS

Guitar Chord Songbook

80 favorite carols for guitarists who just need the lyrics and chords: Angels We Have Heard on High • Away in a Manger • Deck the Hall • Good King Wenceslas • The Holly and the Ivy • Irish Carol • Jingle Bells • Joy to the World • O Holy Night • Rocking • Silent Night • Up on the Housetop • Welsh Carol • What Child Is This? • and more.

00699536 Lyrics/Chord Symbols/
Guitar Chord Diagrams $12.99

CHRISTMAS CAROLS
INCLUDES TAB

Guitar Play-Along Volume 62
Book/CD Pack

8 songs: God Rest Ye Merry, Gentlemen • Hark! The Herald Angels Sing • It Came upon the Midnight Clear • O Come, All Ye Faithful (Adeste Fideles) • O Holy Night • Silent Night • We Three Kings of Orient Are • What Child Is This?

00699798 Guitar Tab $12.95

CHRISTMAS CAROLS
INCLUDES TAB

Jazz Guitar Chord Melody Solos

Chord melody arrangements in notes & tab of 26 songs of the season. Includes: Auld Lang Syne • Deck the Hall • Good King Wenceslas • Here We Come A-Wassailing • Joy to the World • O Little Town of Bethlehem • Toyland • We Three Kings of Orient Are • and more.

00701697 Solo Guitar $12.99

THE CHRISTMAS GUITAR COLLECTION
INCLUDES TAB

Book/CD Pack

20 beautiful fingerstyle arrangements of contemporary Christmas favorites, including: Blue Christmas • Feliz Navidad • Happy Xmas (War Is Over) • I Saw Mommy Kissing Santa Claus • I'll Be Home for Christmas • A Marshmallow World • The Most Wonderful Time of the Year • What Are You Doing New Year's Eve? • and more. CD includes full demos of each piece.

00700181 Fingerstyle Guitar $17.95

CLASSICAL GUITAR CHRISTMAS COLLECTION
INCLUDES TAB

Includes classical guitar arrangements in standard notation and tablature for more than two dozen beloved carols: Angels We Have Heard on High • Auld Lang Syne • Ave Maria • Away in a Manger • Canon in D • The First Noel • I Saw Three Ships • Joy to the World • O Christmas Tree • O Holy Night • Silent Night • What Child Is This? • and more.

00699493 Guitar Solo............................$10.99

FINGERPICKING CHRISTMAS
INCLUDES TAB

Features 20 classic carols for the intermediate-level guitarist. Includes: Away in a Manger • Deck the Hall • The First Noel • It Came upon the Midnight Clear • Jingle Bells • O Come, All Ye Faithful • Silent Night • We Wish You a Merry Christmas • What Child Is This? • and more.

00699599 Solo Guitar............................$9.99

FINGERPICKING YULETIDE
INCLUDES TAB

Carefully written for intermediate-level guitarists, this collection includes an introduction to fingerstyle guitar and 16 holiday favorites: Do You Hear What I Hear • Happy Xmas (War Is Over) • A Holly Jolly Christmas • Jingle-Bell Rock • Rudolph the Red-Nosed Reindeer • and more.

00699654 Fingerstyle Guitar $9.99

FIRST 50 CHRISTMAS CAROLS YOU SHOULD PLAY ON GUITAR
INCLUDES TAB

Accessible, must-know Christmas songs are included in this collection arranged for guitar solo with a combo of tab, chords and lyrics. Includes: Angels We Have Heard on High • The First Noel • God Rest Ye Merry, Gentlemen • The Holly and the Ivy • O Christmas Tree • Silent Night • Up on the Housetop • What Child Is This? • and more.

00236224 Guitar Solo............................$12.99

THE ULTIMATE CHRISTMAS GUITAR SONGBOOK

100 songs in a variety of notation styles, from easy guitar and classical guitar arrangements to note-for-note guitar tab transcriptions. Includes: All Through the Night • Auld Lang Syne • Away in a Manger • Blue Christmas • The Chipmunk Song • The Gift • I've Got My Love to Keep Me Warm • Jingle Bells • One Bright Star • Santa Baby • Silver Bells • Wonderful Christmastime • and more.

00700185 Multi-Arrangements...............$19.95

www.halleonard.com
Prices, contents and availability subject to change without notice.

0518

JAZZ GUITAR CHORD MELODY SOLOS

This series features chord melody arrangements in standard notation and tablature of songs for intermediate guitarists. **INCLUDES TAB**

ALL-TIME STANDARDS

27 songs, including: All of Me • Bewitched • Come Fly with Me • A Fine Romance • Georgia on My Mind • How High the Moon • I'll Never Smile Again • I've Got You Under My Skin • It's De-Lovely • It's Only a Paper Moon • My Romance • Satin Doll • The Surrey with the Fringe on Top • Yesterdays • and more.

00699757 Solo Guitar...................$15.99

IRVING BERLIN

27 songs, including: Alexander's Ragtime Band • Always • Blue Skies • Cheek to Cheek • Easter Parade • Happy Holiday • Heat Wave • How Deep Is the Ocean • Puttin' On the Ritz • Remember • They Say It's Wonderful • What'll I Do? • White Christmas • and more.

00700637 Solo Guitar...................$14.99

CHRISTMAS CAROLS

26 songs, including: Auld Lang Syne • Away in a Manger • Deck the Hall • God Rest Ye Merry, Gentlemen • Good King Wenceslas • Here We Come A-Wassailing • It Came upon the Midnight Clear • Joy to the World • O Holy Night • O Little Town of Bethlehem • Silent Night • Toyland • We Three Kings of Orient Are • and more.

00701697 Solo Guitar...................$12.99

CHRISTMAS JAZZ

21 songs, including Auld Lang Syne • Baby, It's Cold Outside • Cool Yule • Have Yourself a Merry Little Christmas • I've Got My Love to Keep Me Warm • Mary, Did You Know? • Santa Baby • Sleigh Ride • White Christmas • Winter Wonderland • and more.

00171334 Solo Guitar...................$14.99

DISNEY SONGS

27 songs, including: Beauty and the Beast • Can You Feel the Love Tonight • Candle on the Water • Colors of the Wind • A Dream Is a Wish Your Heart Makes • Heigh-Ho • Some Day My Prince Will Come • Under the Sea • When You Wish upon a Star • A Whole New World (Aladdin's Theme) • Zip-A-Dee-Doo-Dah • and more.

00701902 Solo Guitar...................$14.99

DUKE ELLINGTON

25 songs, including: C-Jam Blues • Caravan • Do Nothin' Till You Hear from Me • Don't Get Around Much Anymore • I Got It Bad and That Ain't Good • I'm Just a Lucky So and So • In a Sentimental Mood • It Don't Mean a Thing (If It Ain't Got That Swing) • Mood Indigo • Perdido • Prelude to a Kiss • Satin Doll • and more.

00700636 Solo Guitar...................$12.99

FAVORITE STANDARDS

27 songs, including: All the Way • Autumn in New York • Blue Skies • Cheek to Cheek • Don't Get Around Much Anymore • How Deep Is the Ocean • I'll Be Seeing You • Isn't It Romantic? • It Could Happen to You • The Lady Is a Tramp • Moon River • Speak Low • Take the "A" Train • Willow Weep for Me • Witchcraft • and more.

00699756 Solo Guitar...................$14.99

JAZZ BALLADS

27 songs, including: Body and Soul • Darn That Dream • Easy to Love (You'd Be So Easy to Love) • Here's That Rainy Day • In a Sentimental Mood • Misty • My Foolish Heart • My Funny Valentine • The Nearness of You • Stella by Starlight • Time After Time • The Way You Look Tonight • When Sunny Gets Blue • and more.

00699755 Solo Guitar...................$14.99

LATIN STANDARDS

27 Latin favorites, including: Água De Beber (Water to Drink) • Desafinado • The Girl from Ipanema • How Insensitive (Insensatez) • Little Boat • Meditation • One Note Samba (Samba De Uma Nota So) • Poinciana • Quiet Nights of Quiet Stars • Samba De Orfeu • So Nice (Summer Samba) • Wave • and more.

00699754 Solo Guitar...................$14.99

"Well-crafted arrangements that sound great and are still accessible to most players."
– *Guitar Edge* magazine

www.halleonard.com

CLASSICAL GUITAR

PUBLICATIONS FROM HAL LEONARD

HAL•LEONARD®

Visit Hal Leonard Online at **www.halleonard.com**

Prices, contents and availability subject to change without notice.

0719
005